MW00980398

Casualties of Shopping

By Raymie Lee McDonald

Copyright © 2011 by Raymie Lee McDonald

First Edition – June 2011

ISBN

978-1-77067-481-3 (Paperback)

All rights reserved.

No part of this publication may be reproduced in any form, or by any means, electronic or mechanical, including photocopying, recording, or any information browsing, storage, or retrieval system, without permission in writing from the publisher.

Published by:

FriesenPress

Suite 300 – 852 Fort Street
Victoria, BC, Canada V8W 1H8

www.friesenpress.com

Distributed to the trade by The Ingram Book Company

"*Casualties of Shopping*" is a collection of short stories flowing from the prefrontal cortex of a man who finds humor in the pedestrian qualities of the mundane. McDonald is an author who refuses to be encumbered by punctuation in his haste to tell his stories. Delightfully illustrated by Dame Darcy." **-Barbara Manning**

I read this book during a recent hospitalization and can attest to its
power to entertain. **-Neil Hamburger**

Sick, exciting, saturine. Raymie and Darcy are a match made in a catholic basement. **-Lisa Carver**

Reading your stories from a songwriter's point of view; you take a short melody line (the situation) and you riff it and orchestrate it with such enjoyable phrasing and original instrumentation. From a screenwiter's pov; You are artistically fertile. You choose outrageously uncommon subject matter and make perfect sense with it. You have the storyteller's gift. You know how to tell a story. As a reader; You draw me in with the simplicity of the situations you create and then you take a bit of a turn and a dab of twist and before I know it I am involved.
Lots of movement, humor and structure. Excellent writing. **-Harvey Sid Fisher**

I only got two pages into this book before spilling pizza onto it. I hope it's good, otherwise this comment will seem ridiculous. **- JP Incorporated**

50% of the proceeds of this book are going to
The Dr. Peter Foundation of Vancouver B.C

The Dr. Peter AIDS Foundation helps to rebuild lives shattered by HIV/AIDS, addiction, mental illness, poverty, and discrimination. The combined Day Health Program and 24-hour nursing care Residence at the Dr. Peter Centre is truly unique in Canada – an innovative, comprehensive model of care that is improving people's health and inspiring health care providers around the world.

SUPPORT:

Dame Darcy
Kyla McDonald
Mal Hoskin
Greg Jackson

INSPIRATION:

Irene Hoskin
Emily Horn
Chantal Lemire
Vivian Stanshall
Hilaire Belloc
Maddelin "Lolita" Slayer (of men)

In a sense, you all wrote this book - but in a much larger sense, I did. Now read on...dot dot dot.

Table of Contents

Peter Struck Lorie

Peter Struck Lorie

Peter and Lorie were at their local grocery store doing their groceries for that month, a practice that only worked if a month were two weeks; which it never was. Everything seemed to be running pretty much as usual when all of a sudden Peter struck Lorie right in the head with a frozen turkey. No one had suspected a thing, Peter waited until the aisle they were in had been completely emptied and when it finally was, WHAM, right between the eyes. If the blow had left her conscious she would really be feeling that right about now. When Lorie fell backward and her head hit the floor Peter grabbed hold of the grocery cart handle from where Lorie's hands were placed and proceeded to shop on as though nothing had happened, which is of course the correct procedure to apply when trying to look innocent. You know Peter doesn't even like turkey and that could quite possibly be the real crime here. When he was done with the frozen turkey he quickly discarded it amongst the pile of other frozen turkeys, he's not even going to pay for it, the turkey that is.

As Peter shops he hears a woman scream from a few aisles away and a few seconds after that the call comes in over the intercom "Clean up in aisle ten". Well it appears as though Peter has gotten away with this one. Boy, he sure is an idiot; Peter and Lorie were going to throw a big thanksgiving party just a few nights following this shopping incident. Whether this party will go ahead as planned is hard to say but speaking as the writer I have a sneaking suspicion that it will. Not only was Peter a possible (even a writer must remain objective because even though I know damn well what I wrote and was thinking at the time I could decide to go another way later on, we're a fickle bunch that way) wife murderer, he couldn't even make a peanut butter sandwich, it was really quite pathetic. Lorie had complained bitterly of having to buy stove top stuffing and there was of course the yearly dispute over the outrageous price of canned yams. I guess she whined about it one too many times because there she was alright, colder than...something that is very cold in any event. And the blood that was beginning to ooze out of her, I can't forget to mention the blood, boy was

it gross. As you can imagine (or can't because frankly who wants to) Peter was feeling pretty satisfied with his work perhaps even a bit proud, he figured that not everyone would have the courage to do what he did. The employees at the grocery store made great strides to assure customers that everything was alright while at the same time trying to convince them that it wasn't their free samples that were in any way responsible.

Peter paid for his groceries (after all he's not totally without a conscience) and left the store with fresh new things on his mind, after all he had a thanksgiving party to plan. The day before the party Peter had gotten word that Lorie had died which was pretty much what he was going for when he delivered the blow but now that it was actually done it somehow seemed less satisfying. He couldn't understand why he felt this way; this was something he has been working up enough nerve to do for years. It seems that Lorie was one step ahead of Peter even in death. Here it is another Thanksgiving and nothing to be thankful for in sight.

The

Clotheshorse

The Clotheshorse

It was Labor Day weekend again for Janet and her sister Kate and for everybody else for that matter but for Janet and Kate it was a particularly stressful time. Yet another year of school was looming around the corner, to them it was quite a gloomy prospect indeed. Janet and Kate were twins and they were both going to be going into grade eleven which now made them seniors but also embedded in them the "I'm going to make the life of everyone around me a living hell" attitude. Like a lot of school girls they had certain affection for clothes shopping, couldn't get enough of it and the mall was kind of like their home away from home. As the first day of school grew ever more closer they both decided to set aside some time to get their new fall wardrobes because god forbid their friends should see them in anything more than once at any given time. Besides the thrill of shopping for just the right accessories at a great deal was such a rush it almost made the upcoming school year more bearable...almost.

Janet and Kate dragged themselves into every clothing store that was in their local mall looking for just the right things to become the envy of their friends and of course to attract the male element. As far as they were concerned the education end of it was just something that got in the way of those more important pursuits. The most crucial thing though about this whole shopping experience was that the two of them get completely different outfits, they both felt that the stigma attached to twins liking to dress alike was completely ridiculous, it was always something that they despised. When they were younger and family members used to dress them the same because they thought they looked "so adorable" Janet and Kate would always lock themselves in their room until either their parents told them they could change or they were offered money, but unfortunately they were rarely that "adorable".

In some big department store I can't remember the name of (as the writer I really remember quite clearly but there is no point in getting them involved) is where it all took place. Janet and Kate were in the fitting room trying on some

things that they had picked out for themselves, none of which were going to look good once they got home but in the right lighting and in front of the specially enhanced imaging of the store's mirrors they were real gems.

"Hey, I believe that I had my eye on that outfit first", Kate was quick to speak up when she saw her outfit being taken away from her.

"So you will just have to pick out a new one", Janet halfheartedly knew that her sister wasn't just going to sit idly by and accept that poor excuse for an argument but it was out of her mouth before she had time to think. The two of them argued about it for awhile, obviously not realizing how truly petty the argument was. When Janet finally came to this realization she failed to inform Kate of her new found awareness and instead decided to just take the outfit to the change room and proceeded to try it on without the improper closure such an argument like this deserves. I guess Janet wasn't aware as to what extent Kate was willing to go to look as good as she possibly could because as they stood in the change room together staring in to the mirror at how Janet looked in the item that caused so much stress between the two of them, a wave of jealousy washed over Kate. As Janet began to change back into her original clothing, Kate suddenly flew into a violent and clearly unprovoked (at least as far as Janet was concerned) rage. Kate strangled her sister with her own brassier (the ultimate insult as far as I'm concerned) and after that decided to try on the dress herself; ill gotten gains not withstanding, it couldn't be denied...she looked fabulous. In a moment of clarity she finally took her attention off the dress and placed it on her sister, who lay there motionless.

What Kate failed to realize was how she was going to get out of this small dressing room without letting people know what she had done. She couldn't decide though if she cared more about people finding out what she had done or the pathetic reason why she did it, even she could see how stupid it was but it was a momentary impulse and one that can't easily be taken back. Kate decided to follow that age old practice of crawling under the door, just as so many juvenile high school students crawling under locked bathroom stalls as a way of trying to one up their peers by making them practice the noble art of bladder control. Kate felt that under the door was the best way to go because this way the door will stay locked and nobody will discover Janet for awhile, once again silly high school antics show us the way. Kate knew that she would have to move extremely fast; just slipping out the door would have been hard enough. She listened at the door for voices and peeked through the cracks, waiting for customers and salespeople to leave. After everybody left the vicinity, Kate, with dress in hand, crouched down and attempted to get into some kind of small ball with her knees touching her chest, arms tucked in, dress clenched in her fist with the end of it draped out behind her. She began to roll, as she did the top part of her butt hit the top of the door which made her momentarily nervous so she quickly fell to her stomach and she scrambled out of there. As she was making her departure the part of her dress that was sticking out was sticking out just enough that during the roll it flew up and hooked on to some sort of edge which caused a fairly extensive tear in the material. When Kate got up off the ground she noticed the damage at which point she realized that this was probably an indication of the kind of school year to come.

Bone Crushing Night on the Town

Bone Crushing Night
On The Town

It all started innocently enough with a homely looking guy named Ted who had absolutely nothing to do on a Saturday night but had lots of gas in his car to do it with. He felt as though he had to be doing anything other than sitting at home for one more night massaging his mother's feet so instead he decided to get in his car and drive around aimlessly until something just came to him. While he was out there he entertained the notion of going to his friends' houses (homely people need friends too) to see what was going on there and to see if he could gather up anymore people for his little road trip. Most of his friends did seem to legitimately have plans already because Ted did not see them in the house during his impromptu visit with all of their mothers. That is why spontaneous visits are better than phone calls because it is easy to lie on the phone about your degree of availability whereas in person anyone can see that you are doing nothing. Ted was able to find two of his friends that weren't busy and after a brief period of negotiations he was able to convince them that cruising around on a Saturday night was the thing to be doing. The two friends that Ted was able to gather up were not too hard to convince as they were as unpopular as Ted was. Steve, a pimply faced nineteen year old who just graduated from high school and also just got his drivers license and the other was a college student named Dan who couldn't stay in a dorm because he lacked the certain social skills that put him in contention for such perks.

Once all three of them were assembled they were ready to begin their wild night of whatever the hell they were going to do. Ted started driving, almost hitting things while trying to make last minute decisions about where exactly he was headed. They hit all the good evening spots: the beach, the park, took a walk through the graveyard because one of them heard somewhere that hanging out with the dead was a pretty hip thing to be doing. They even tried to sneak into a

movie but Dan began to sweat profusely and it was making him uncomfortable so they had to put the kibosh on that.

"Hey Ted", Steve's pathetic voice came from the back seat, "I just got my driver's license but I don't have a car yet so can I drive?".

Ted pondered the question over and over looking for an easy way to say no. "Look, I don't doubt the fact that you're an excellent driver I just haven't been driving that long myself and insurance is expensive enough without having an accident on my record from the get go".

"Come on", Steve pleaded, "I promise that you and your car will be in good hands".

"Well if you promise I guess my hands are tied", Ted said sarcastically. So Ted pulled over and removed himself from the driver's seat and walked over to Steve's passenger door and opened it, "alright, but for god sakes be careful".

"Thanks, you won't regret this".

"Oh, I'm pretty sure that I will", Ted moaned.

Steve slid into the driver's seat feeling on top of the world with his new found "no one's going to fuck with me now" attitude, nothing that a few hours in rush hour traffic won't cure. Steve drove around successfully for the remainder of the evening and it looked as if the casualties were going to be kept to a minimum. Having said that we now join Ted on the next page, who is getting hungry. Take it away.

Ted: "Are you guys hungry? I'm hungry, hey Steve, drive through the McDonald's drive thru and we will just grab a few burgers or something".

Steve and Dan both thought that sounded like a really good idea so as soon as Steve saw a McDonalds in sight he pulled into the drive thru where they ordered and started to move accordingly. Halfway through the lineup Ted's car ran out of gas which surprised all three of them and at first they really weren't sure what to make of it or how to handle it. In the drive thru there were about three or four cars ahead of them but nobody waiting behind them so it looked like they were going to have to push it out and if they could do that there was a gas station right in the same lot as McDonalds. Ted got out of the back seat and went around to the trunk to see if he had a gas can because then he could just run over to the gas station. Just as Ted went to do this Steve put the car in reverse, got out and asked the driver ahead of them to help back them out using his car. The driver of the car agreed and they were on their way. Steve went to tell the other two the good news but as Steve made his way to the others, the driver of the car ahead of them started too early. Before Steve could tell the others of this great plan he had, the front bumper of Ted's car was pushed against a good amount by the back bumper of the heavily revving car in front. Ted, with his head still buried in his trunk definitely wasn't ready for his car to attack him the way it did and within a matter of seconds Ted was swept under the wheels. Closer consultation was obviously needed here between all the parties involved but on the upside (if you had to go looking for one) the car was free from the drive thru. Steve felt responsible (more so than anyone else) so he thought the least he could do was pay for the gas (the ironic thing is that if you had a hand in running over your best friend in his own car, buying his gas is probably the least you could do).

Well, it had been a pretty eventful night but not one they would soon tell anyone about because it sounded too embarrassing. Steve imagined that Ted wouldn't ever mention it; no one wants to tell people they were hit by a car that had no gas and was rolling back. Steve figured that he couldn't drive Ted's car home because his mother would ask too many questions so in an act of desperation Steve parked Ted's car in the parking lot and placed Ted's body in the front seat and make it look like he was waiting for someone in McDonalds. Ted was still out cold (but breathing) and when he did come to he looked like he was only going to have a few bruises. Once Steve and Dan were satisfied with how Ted looked they began to walk home. They felt so guilty that they vowed not to talk to Ted for quite awhile and when Ted comes to I think he will find that the feeling is entirely mutual.

Don't
Do It Yourself

Don't Do It Yourself

The thought of redecorating the house filled Nancy's very soul with an unquenchable longing; a longing for someone else to do it if the truth be known because it was one of those things that you know has to be done but something you dread doing nonetheless. Nancy was a procrastinator. And like any good procrastinator she had a habit of saying she was going to do something then pushing the project back until it ended up not getting done at all; a fact...or just a definition of procrastinate, either way, vocabulary lessons aside, this was going to be the day that it all happened.

Nancy was waiting for her husband Sidney to actually start this undertaking but after months of watching Sidney sit around on the couch watching television with a beer in his hand she decided that, left in his hands it wasn't going to be done anytime too soon. Sidney always meant to get started but it felt like baseball season got longer and longer each year which would inevitably lead to football, there was the whole hockey issue and basketball he had never been interested in but he had heard good things as of late. Besides, Sidney's contention, as pathetic as it was, was that the woman's liberation movement was never quite able to make that final leap into the area of home maintenance. And as of then the gauntlet had been thrown down so Nancy of course felt she naturally had to pick it up for all of women kind. Sidney might have been a couch potato but he was no stranger to reverse psychology.

The years of moving furniture and appliances like old and new washers and dryers through the house had caused chips in the drywall and large rips in the wallpaper which couldn't really be hidden anymore with a simple picture or some well placed pieces of furniture. Public television proved to be somewhat of a good teacher in home renovation as well. She watched programs about redoing your bathroom, painting the interior and exterior of your house, amateur plumbing and other things that would usually be as boring as hell except of course when you can make good use of it, like now for instance, but even then it was a struggle for Nancy to stay awake. During the next few weeks Nancy measured walls and toured her local hardware and do-it-yourself stores buying all the tools she would need to do this little project. Something Nancy found helpful as well was that at these stores they would show these little promotional videos of products that the store sells and how to use them, the caulking video was her favorite and sometimes she found it tough to pull herself away, what made it better and more interesting than public television is anybody's guess.

As far as a fresh coat of paint went, she looked at swatches and swatches of every color imaginable, who knew there were so many different shades of white. Nancy had trouble deciding what to wear in the morning so a choice like this that you will have to put up with and see everyday is a truly tough one to make. She tried to choose a color that best went with her furniture while at the same time trying to choose one that relatively matched a majority of Sidney's clothing since he would spend so much time watching TV and falling asleep on the couch, it seemed only natural that Sidney try to blend in as best as he could. To further illustrate this point, as Nancy looked at each paint swatch she would pull out this picture of Sidney sleeping on the couch that she had taken the night before and would hold it up to each sample so she could examine whether or not they did indeed blend well with each other. After going through countless books she did find one that camouflaged Sidney quite well, to the unfocussed eye you would swear that you could see that Sidney was just a disembodied head so needless to say (but I will say it anyway) that was the one.

Why was it that anything that Nancy ever chose was the most expensive and it had to be special ordered? Nancy wondered if that was some sort of chapter in Murphy's Law that people always forget about and if it's not it should be. While she waited for the paint to come in she went home to try and scrape the existing wallpaper off the wall which actually proved to be quite a task in itself that had to be spaced out over a few days. What made it an arduous process was the fact that it was only her doing it. But she was okay with doing it alone because although she did love Sidney she knew that he would be somewhat useless and more of a hindrance than a help. Every once in a while he would say, "Is there anything I can do to help?". But when she would start to answer, trying to take him up on his hollow gesture and give him some sort of meaningless job she would turn around and see that he would be staring at the TV like a zombie, probably unaware that he had even asked, so she never bothered to answer him.

They were planning to throw a Thanksgiving Day party being that Thanksgiving was just a few days away but now that Nancy's house was a mess it was going to be impossible to have guests over. Nancy did realize that she could have started all this redecorating after Thanksgiving but she also knew that you have to do these kinds of things when the mood strikes you or you will never get them done, especially if you really don't want to do them in the first place. As it turned out, after many a phone call, Thanksgiving dinner was successfully moved to her friend Lorie and her husband Peter's house.

She hadn't even begun to scratch the surface yet but she felt she was doing really well for an amateur and she even began to think that maybe she had a new career on her hands...or at least a first career. Upon peeling back the old, faded wallpaper Nancy discovered all sorts of drawings and graffiti that seemed to point to the fact that the people that lived there before them were deeply demented and disturbed people and quite coincidentally were invited to the very same Thanksgiving party that Nancy was supposed to be throwing and now her friend Lorie was throwing which made Nancy have second thoughts about whether her and Sidney should go. Just then Sidney got up and his eyes fell upon the graffiti and immediately he began to remind Nancy of the night years ago that they got really drunk and went wild and tore down the existing wallpaper (the wallpaper that was up before the stuff Nancy just tore down herself), drew all over the particle board and re-wallpapered; good times indeed. Although she didn't have any recollection of that night whatsoever, she couldn't deny that it happened simply because she even did boring things in a drunken stupor; the only good thing that came out of it was that she, simply by accident, realized that she was better at wallpapering than she thought. This also meant that Sydney and Nancy were now free to go to the Thanksgiving dinner without fear of being embarrassed when they run into the people who drew those perverted drawings because it was them.

When the home improvement store called to tell Nancy her paint came in she was excited, which tells you a little about how fulfilling her life is, but nevertheless she was ready to get cracking. Speaking of cracking, when Nancy arrived at the store to pick up the stuff that was waiting for her she shopped a little for other supplies she might need, that is when the bathtub fell on her. It was laying against the wall on the highest shelf, propped up there with a few pieces of wood holding it in place, or so it would seem, and it came sliding down just like a championship bobsledder...if they were riding in a bathtub which isn't really a bad idea. Nancy was of course knocked cold and it couldn't have been a good advertisement for business so the employees of the store all descended on Nancy to try and get her to the back of the store where they called for an ambulance.

It wasn't yet clear as to how serious Nancy's condition was but it almost gave fellow customers a heart attack and some of them ran screaming out of the store in a mad frenzy at what they had just witnessed. Sidney hadn't been notified yet and how would he take it is anybody's guess. The big question still needed to be addressed: Would Sidney attempt to finish the redecorating job himself? Being the trooper that Nancy is she would want him to continue on with the project and put it ahead of her own condition but we all know he won't.

One-Sided Arguement

One Sided Arguement

It all started innocently enough with a young boy's love for music and from there it ricocheted into a...well...something much more. A story that waffles between good friendship and sheer hatred and animosity. A story that is reminiscent of everyday life while at the same time being something so far fetched it's not even funny. This story belongs to a boy of seventeen who we will call Tom, not for reasons that would put him in any danger if this story were to get out, on the contrary, for that was his name. Tom had a good part-time job at a reputable company quite nearby to were he lived in his hometown of Anywhere, Canada (sister city to that famous burg in certain fictional stories Anywhere, USA). Tom made good money there but he was always broke and a major reason for this was that he loved listening to music, going to concerts and buying the latest compact discs. Even he himself could not believe how addictive this practice could be. It was like smoking or drinking but less destructive, but then again with so many bands pushing the boundaries of good taste and decency maybe not.

Eventually the day came when Tom owned all the music that he had ever wanted. He usually kept lists of things he had wanted that he either had a good feeling about or that he had read a review of somewhere, and each time he bought one he would scratch that one off his list. After he had accumulated all the music he wished to own he had nowhere else to direct his income because he still lived with his parents and he didn't go on may dates so he started directing his attention towards sending away for free catalogues of other C.D.'s he could get, he particularly focused on record companies that were home to his favorite bands. This was where all his problems really began.

Most record companies had the same drill whereby they would usually send Tom a big list of what he had to choose from, maybe with a little critique of each one (as if they were ever going to give a negative review of their own stuff) and a list of prices at the back. The majority of the companies he got stuff from were really nice about everything, they were prompt with shipping (Tom liked the obscure and was probably asking for the crap they were dying to unload) and if they were temporarily out of that item they would send him something else for bearing with them, not a lavish gift but it showed they cared about their customers. For the most part Tom was enjoying what he was getting from these companies but one day he sent away for a few things from a record company we will call "Straight As An Octopus Records", because that was their name. That is officially when, unknown to Tom at the time, the music industry broke his heart (Tom was very emotional and tended to be a bit over dramatic). Tom had sent away for three items: two C.D.'s and a poster and that's it because, although he was pretty sure what he was getting, there was still a slight chance that he wouldn't like it that much. He waited and waited. Everyday after work he would rush to his mailbox in anticipation that his order would be there but it never was. For the next little while the hope of getting what he had ordered was the focus of all his attention; pretty pathetic but at the same time if this is the only major concern in his life he's not doing too badly. The day that it did come was, in Tom's mind at any rate, a momentous occasion (which is yet another peak into Tom's exciting life). Upon inspection of the package containing his order he found that it wasn't as it should be and would soon lead to the end of his mail ordering days and dare I say the breakdown of the fabric of our society; but let's see, I'm getting ahead of myself here.

When Tom opened the mailbox he expected a small package but instead he got a card informing him that his package was at the post office which was of course fair enough because he figured that the poster was rolled up instead of folded so it wouldn't fit in the mailbox, a wise practice and nothing to think anything of at the time. The next day when Tom went to the post office to pick up his package; there was a tube waiting for him that would hold a poster but that was it, nothing attached to it that would vaguely resemble a compact disc sort of shape. Tom looked at the card that was placed in his mailbox and it did indeed say that there was only one package and even inquired at the postal counter if there had been a mistake but unfortunately there was none. On the way home Tom was hoping that the compact discs were either pretty damn small or that it was some kind of trick packaging on the part of the record company. Later that night Tom opened up his package where he found the poster he had ordered, a slip of paper listing what he got and what he didn't get and a small letter that read:

We are temporarily out of stock of the two C.D.'s you are requesting. Please reorder in two months or so. Please use the slip of paper enclosed as a receipt when reordering so you are not charged again.

Signed,

Dan Gregory

Tom's first thought after reading the very informal letter was who is this Dan guy? Tom knew of the guy that ran this particular record company because it was the same guy who was the singer of his favorite band which encouraged him to write to that company in the first place. If there was any problem Tom would have thought that the person running the company would want to solve it and not this Dan Bozo.

Tom felt a bit cheated but he thought that he would just chalk that up to anticipation. He decided he would wait and try again in a few months as the letter specified which is probably a good idea considering that there wasn't a whole lot he could do; if something is not available it's just not available. When Tom did try back again he assumed that it was, in fact as they said, and the items that Tom had requested would now be there so without any thought at all he sent his receipt back to them and left it at that. Tom waited and waited for his package a second time or at least any kind of reply at all from the company but nothing was forthcoming. After a few more months went by Tom decided to compose a letter that would surely have immediate and direct results, words that would have a debilitating effect on the most unscrupulous of wrongdoers. Tom didn't get too chatty he just got right to the point while at the same time trying to sound pleasant:

To Whom It May Concern,

Four months ago I ordered two CDs and a poster. I was sent the poster with a note/receipt showing that I was owed the two CDs still because I was told that you were out of stock at the time and to try back in two months. Two months ago I sent the note/receipt back to you so I could claim the CDs I was entitled to. I would greatly appreciate it if you could send the CDs or some sort of explanation as to what's going on. As of the date of this letter it has been another month and a half since I sent the note/receipt back to you so if the CDs are in the mail please disregard this letter.

Thank you.

Signed,

Tom Jarvis

After Tom finished writing the letter he wasn't too sure if he was comfortable with what he had wrote or not. On the one hand he wanted his compact discs but on the other hand he didn't want to come off as a complete dink. In the end he decided that it was probably okay and he stuck the letter in an envelope and quickly mailed it before he had any second thoughts. Tom waited for another three months and absolutely no reply in sight. He was starting to wonder what kind of Mickey Mouse operation they were running there anyway and was this a run of the mill scam they eventually perpetrated on everyone once they had gained their trust or was this something personal? Tom knew he was wasting his time with these guys but for whatever reason, reasons only known to him, he decided to write another letter. In this letter he decided to try and sound a bit less formal, perhaps giving the impression that he was getting agitated by the situation. In his heart of hearts he knew that he was never going to see those CD's or some type of refund so this second letter in a sense was just to blow off a little steam:

To whom is likely to care,

Many moons ago I ordered some stuff from you guys and it still ceases to be in my possession. At the time I ordered it you did not have it available so you sent me some sort of rain check thing and told me to try back in two months. Well what can I tell you, nothing came of it. I suppose (in some small sense) I am to blame because a) I could have ordered it from my local record store and let them deal with you or b) I should have made a copy of that rain check thing to keep continually holding over your head, not that it seems to have an effect on you anyways. I have written you a letter about this matter already and can assume by the response I got that it must have successfully found its way into the trash. I must tell you that I am not expecting your package anytime soon so in this, my second letter, I am just letting you know that you have lost yourself a customer.

I am sure that this will not affect your business in the least but I for one feel vindicated.

Yours disapprovingly,

Tom Jarvis

After Tom mailed the letter he felt better, he felt as though he really had had the last laugh and although he ended up not getting anything for his troubles he did learn a valuable lesson. He never again ordered anything through the mail and for all he knows his package of CD's could actually be out there in Canada Post limbo. That would be a good ending if it were over but the bad feelings manifest themselves.

...

It is now a year and a half later and Tom is reading the paper one night and sees that David Bradley, one of Tom's favorite singers and coincidently the guy who runs "Straight As An Octopus Records", is coming to town. Tom had forgotten, for the most part, all about what had happened to him but news of this visit made all the memories of his bad experience come flooding back to him. Tom began to assume that David Bradley coming to town was some sort of sign not to let this thing rest. David Bradley was apparently coming to the local university to give a lecture or something because when he wasn't touring with his band he was doing this spoken word/poetry kind of thing. After work one day Tom went to buy himself a ticket to this show thinking that he was going to have this big, elaborate confrontational thing that was going to result in nothing but a beg for forgiveness.

The night of the show Tom sat in the auditorium bored out of his mind, it was like sitting through a political science class but a really boring one. Half the things he was saying weren't that interesting and it was probable that he was lying, you could really disprove him if you wanted to but the occasional story he told was interesting. At intermission Tom was walking around outside the auditorium doors when he spotted a woman who looked like some kind of public relations person, Tom didn't know much about public relations he just had a feeling and the fact that she was dressed better than anyone else there didn't hurt either.

"Excuse me but are you with David Bradley by any chance?", Tom looked at her hopefully. She looked at Tom as if she already knew what Tom was going to say, "Yes I am", she said, "I am his PR person, is there a problem?".

"No...no", Tom said, "I just wanted to know if I could talk to David Bradley for a minute after the show".

"Well we can't really do that but afterwards he will be hanging back to sign things for people so you can probably try and talk to him then but I don't know how successful you will be". Tom thanked her and opened the doors of the auditorium to a crowd of people waiting patiently in their seats for the speaker to return to the stage. As the lights went down and the crowd started to hush Tom laid back in his seat and got ready for another hour of this guys excessive blathering and hoped that he wasn't sitting there for nothing. When the show finally let out, the large crowd of people left their seats and started heading towards another part of the building where they gathered around a small table that David Bradley was already sitting at ready to sign whatever paraphernalia people had for him to sign. Tom couldn't believe how pushy this get together was going to be, everyone trying to position themselves so that their particular item gets signed. Some people just wanted to be able to talk to David Bradley to tell him how great he was, or in Tom's case, to accuse him of fraud (Tom was pretty sure he was the only one there to do that). Most people brought the usual things to get signed: old records he made, CDs, magazines he'd done interviews in. Tom

hoped that someone would have the foresight to point out to Mr. Bradley that he should stick to singing because the stuff that night was really bad. When Tom finally strong armed his way to the front of the crowd and faced the source of his troubles he spoke as if this guy was really going to know or care who Tom was, "Excuse me Mr. Bradley but my name is Tom Jarvis and I am a big fan but I am having trouble with your record label right now and I am wondering if you can assist me in any way?", Tom asked a bit nervously. "At the moment I am a bit busy, as you can see, to help you out with anything like that but if you write a letter to my record label I'm sure they will help you out alright". Upon hearing the end of the conversation someone else barged up to the front to get to the table. Tom thought awhile about the response he got, "send a letter", he said again to himself. And with that he flung himself to the front once again and over the table into the performer and knocked him to the ground. Everyone in the crowd rushed forward and formed a circle around the two, with Tom lying sideways across the crushed body. As security came to fetch Tom, he just thought about how this would probably affect his dealings with record companies in the future.

Murial's Burial

Murial's Burial

They were dropping like flies at the old age home where Kimberley Brewer's mother took up residence in a last ditch effort to claim independence and show her daughter that she still had her wits about her. The irony of course was that even there it seemed as though they were under constant house arrest and sometimes treated as small children, but one man's freedom is another man's prison and vice versa. Kimberley Brewer was a self important busybody who fancied herself as somewhat of an important person around town and it wasn't as if she didn't love her mother, she did, she just loved her more in small increments. Sometimes Kimberley would come by the home and pick her mother up and take her on trips and things just to make it seem as though she wasn't sweeping her under the rug entirely, although, quite frankly, who's kidding who. It's not all as pathetic as it seems though, I mean the home was close to the downtown strip and the residents were allowed to enter and leave of their own volition. Everyone who lived there seemed genuinely happy on the whole so they were all pretty disappointed when they began to hear of the mysterious deaths that were occurring. Now death can take many forms and when you are in your senior years it's more probable that it could rear it's ugly head at any time.

This particular old age home was just like any other one in that most deaths were of natural causes that happened peacefully during the night or something to that affect which, in my opinion, is the nicest way to go. The deaths as of late were very mysterious indeed, not mysterious in the conventional way; such as having a killer on the loose and no one knows who it is, but rather deaths that occur as accidents that are so bizarre that it seems as though there is a curse on that person. These deaths either transpired as a result of careless mistakes like mixing rat poison in with the food which, as anyone working there would testify, was a freak thing or they actually have a very funny story behind them. Or falling down a garbage shoot and from there….well…the details are a bit gruesome after that but suffice to say; if you wish to pay your last respects you might as well drop off a few bags of garbage while you are there.

One of the oddest deaths occurred during variety show that was known to frequent the local senior centers and retirement homes in the area. It was like anything else that was put in place to make the old and decrepits' life more fulfilling; visits from cub scouts, brownies, having arts and crafts, going on field trips, you name it. Sometimes a visit from a family member could be a bit of a wait but it's not because they didn't love them, or maybe it was, it's just for the most part no one wants to have to live with or take care of their parents when they become too dependent, which is of course selfish and very ironic. The much lighter reason for placing your parents in a home are that when they are out of sight they are out of mind which is an okay excuse (still sort of callous) except it basically reduces your parents to a misplaced baseball glove that is just forgotten about. The really cold sons and daughters of these seniors are the ones who have the gall to leave a message with the retirement home staff for their parents telling them that they wish they could be there today. Getting back to the variety show where upon the most bizarre death of them all transpired, it was during the magic portion of the show where a volunteer, an elderly woman with glasses who could barely walk was placed in a box and sawed in half. The first part of the trick was pretty impressive, the second part not so much. The one positive thing you can say about the trick was that it was quick and painless; as for the audience on hand that witnessed the event it sent them screaming from their seats.

Kimberley Brewer had been invited to some sort of Thanksgiving party/ dinner thing by a coworker of hers named Peter and she decided to invite her mother to get her out and about, which is nice but fails to notify the host of this plan. One unexpected person at a party can really put a damper on dinner, especially when there isn't enough, it can be awkward. It just so happens that Kimberley's mother, whose name was Murial, had died on the very day that Kimberley came to pick her up for the dinner/party. Murial had not gone in the usual bizarre way that was so timely at the home as of late; this death was of natural causes and happened during a lawn bowling tournament where the physical exertion must have been too much. It was either that or someone on an opposing team did her in; you know how competitive lawn bowling can be. As soon as Kimberley had found out her mother had died she took the next logical step and phoned the bank to stop payment on the checks that paid for the retirement home and once that was taken care of she was able to begin the mourning process. Kimberley and her ex-husband Todd began the tedious task of planning a funeral for Murial which Kimberley insisted on doing but in all honesty it turned out to be more trouble than it was worth. Kimberley and her ex-husband didn't get along at all but he wanted to help with the arrangements because he always got along with Murial really well, to the point where she treated him like her own son. Kimberley was quite willing to let Todd help because she didn't deal with death all that well, besides the fact that funerals and death in general can be an expensive thing, so even though you may hate someone intensely, if they have money to help out you can overlook that.

Not to downplay the seriousness of it all but Kimberley didn't see why she couldn't just have her mother cremated and be done with it. She wasn't being heartless (as far as she was concerned) she just didn't see the point of dragging it all out and making a big production of it, even though she was doing it because she knew her mother would want her to; if nothing else for the drama. It's morosely ironic though because Kimberley can remember when she was a little girl and her mother used to tell her that once you die people are going to forget you in about two minutes. Why she used to say this is anybody's guess, and especially to a little girl, but it was usually after she had a few drinks. Another reason for the burial was that Murial always used to be emphatic about donating her organs to science. Kimberley could remember when she first got her drivers license her mother pushed her to fill out the organ donor part on the back of the license. "You are always so healthy Kim, why don't you share your gift with others? Money can't buy you happiness but organs can, so try to take your money with you but leave your organs on the other side..."and then she would sort of trail off into a sort of mumble, once again with drink in hand.

It only took one visit to a funeral home to pick out a casket, for some reason Kim thought it would be tougher than it was. She tried to make out like price was no object but when she was browsing through this book with pictures of caskets in it designed to help you make your selection, she got around to asking herself how important is it that a dead person be comfortable and does it really say something about how much you love them? She especially didn't find it necessary to spring for a silk pillow, after all it wasn't as if her mother was going to be watching her funeral from somewhere and thinking to herself "I can't believe they didn't get me a pillow to rest my head. Geese, that really tears it".

Kim and Todd wandered around the funeral parlor looking aimlessly for just the right casket, they actually only had a few choices allotted to them being that Murial was pretty tall and big boned, all and all, a full figured gal. As they lingered, looking for just the right deal (while at the same time trying not to understate class) Todd and Kim began to fight. It all started innocently enough with petty little disagreements and bickering about things as small as what the casket should be made of to all out war over who gets the final word on which one they will finally end up with seeing as how they couldn't come to an agreement between the two of them. They were both stubborn and refused to come to any compromises; the Mortician wanted to offer up his opinion but when he heard one of them say that they couldn't wait to see the other in one of these things he decided to bite his tongue.

After that fight was over and they returned in silence to Kim's house it was time for the next fight to get underway which was sparked by talk of the date of the funeral and in turn brought a temporary standstill to any forthcoming arrangements.

"Why are you so dead set on having this funeral this Sunday? You are of course aware that I coach a little girls' baseball team and this Sunday we are playing for the championship", Todd said to Kim as if she was supposed to have already had that day marked off on her calendar. As soon as Todd relayed this bit of information to Kim it immediately sent her into a tizzy because she couldn't fathom how a baseball game was more important than a funeral (championship or not). Another reason for the tizzy was that when Todd informed Kim of this information he made it sound so much more important than her mother dying. So as soon as Todd was done speaking she immediately went into yelling mode, "Look, the fact is, apart from that lame excuse for trying to re-schedule of all things a funeral, you're my ex-husband which as far as I'm concerned doesn't really commit you to any of this stuff!". The truth of the matter was that the funeral had to be this Sunday because the day after she was going on a vacation to Florida, but she wasn't going to let Todd know that, she wouldn't give him the satisfaction, not after the way she yelled at him.

The date of the funeral remained for when it was originally planned, and Todd decided that he wouldn't go to the funeral because he just couldn't let the kids down, it wasn't their fault that Murial packed it in the way she did and it was true that the kids were going after a championship. It's not like Kim's mom was going to be turning in her grave over the fact that Todd didn't go to her funeral. Todd not attending the funeral was actually a win-win situation as far as Kim was concerned because they fought like cats and dogs all the time and she was sure that a public function (no matter how somber) would be no exception, however, she was still glad that he was willing to pay half the expenses because they were slowly mounting up. The beauty of the way this all turned out (in Kim's mind anyway) was that Todd is paying half the expenses because he feels guilty for not attending even though they are only having it this Sunday in order to cater to the plans of Kim.

Kim never did make a habit of hanging out in graveyards so when it came to the purchasing and scouting locations for Murial's burial plot it was an experience that was a first and hopefully a last. One thing that was very strange about her plot shopping was that she almost forgot to do it; imagine everyone's surprise when, after the funeral, they had nowhere to put the body; Kim thanked her lucky stars she remembered because having to explain her predicament would have been the ultimate embarrassment. But just when you thought they had learned their lesson, Todd and Kim were together again. They got together because Todd's father had died last year so he had a bit of plot buying knowledge (if you can have such a thing) so he swallowed his pride and attempted to lend his assistance (however futile it might be) to the project. Little did they know that this funeral would spontaneously cause one of their own downfalls.

If you are not choosy about where to bury a loved one buying a plot can be easy but if you are particular about where you want them it could be rather difficult, it all depends on whether you mind a long drive just to visit a little square of ground. The reason why you might want to consider this small formality is because it's crowded out there. Some people always refer to the population explosion for all the countries woes what with unwanted babies being born everyday but let me tell you that just as many die. It made Kim realize why people buy their plots well before they die. She always assumed it was so that other people had less to worry about when you pass on or that it was a crappy birthday present but when it came right down to it you pretty well have to buy early so that you can make sure that you get in, just like anything really. When Kim and Todd went to visit a few cemeteries to get an idea of where Kim would be satisfied putting her mother she couldn't believe how close they were putting these headstones, it was almost coming to the point where they were going to have to start throwing bodies together.

As Kim and Todd walked through the cemetery they passed quite a few freshly dug graves with plywood over the top of them obviously waiting for the inhabitants to come and take their rightful place; or to return from having had left, muahaha. In some cases there were a few in a row and it made Kim sigh to think of the entire family that wanted to be buried together, couldn't get that kind of togetherness around Kim's house, Kim's family couldn't wait to get away from each other. The only thing wrong with wanting to be buried together is that they might have had some irreconcilable fight just before they died and it would be too late to get out of being buried beside each other (I am aware that when you are dead you could really care less who is beside you but if you really detest them when you are alive you may have strong feelings on the subject).

Kim did finally get a plot but she had to settle on one in a cemetery clear across town, which remained a very sore subject with her but in the greater scheme of things at least Murial was getting buried as per her wishes. After purchasing the plot, Kim and Todd stood there at the foot of the site with the grounds keeper (propping himself up with a shovel and sweating profusely after just having freshly dug it) discussing it's finer points and general location; seeing as how all the headstones start to look alike after awhile and finding the one you are looking for can be tough. There were some lax moments in the conversation though when they discussed topics that didn't center around death, but considering that they were standing in the middle of a cemetery it was hard to stray too far off the topic of death. The conversation then got to what Murial's tombstone should read and this is where Todd and Kim disagreed (was there any doubt). Kim thought it should remain general, name, life span and a little something about how much she will be missed; Todd agreed with that but he also thought it should say stuff about what kind of person she was and some of the funny stuff she used to say. And that is when Kim started yelling again, "It's just a simple headstone, we're not writing a book of her life here" and after she said that she stuck her fingers in her ears so she couldn't hear his reply. When he tried to remove her fingers from her ears so that he could start yelling he was met with tremendous opposition, an opposition that carried itself into a full fledged attack. Before Todd knew what was happening Kim had spun around and whipped the shovel out from under the groundskeeper which sent him to the ground and started smacking Todd upside the head sharply with the end of it. When Todd finally lay on the ground motionless, Kim removed the piece of plywood covering her mother's freshly dug grave and kicked Todd into it. Before she covered the hole up again she looked at the groundskeeper, shrugged her shoulders and gave him a few hard raps on his head with the end of the shovel and gave him a kick into the hole. She threw the shovel in and covered the plywood over the hole again. As she rose to her feet after laying the plywood down she thought about what a beautiful day it was turning out to be, just the sort of day to pick up an urn for yourself.

Accessory to Murder

Accessory To Murder

Tina was surprised when out of the blue her sister Lorie invited her to a Thanksgiving Day party at her house. She hadn't gotten along too well with her sister in the past and hadn't even spoken to her in quite awhile so naturally she was a bit hesitant but decided that this would be an excellent opportunity to make amends so she thanked her sister and graciously accepted the invitation. The first thing Tina needed was something to wear, she realized that the party wasn't for quite awhile and it was only at her sister's but who knows who you could run into, it could be the next love of your life or a producer who feels you are going to be the next big thing, you've got to be prepared. She was going to try and avoid going shopping if she possibly could because it was something she was addicted to, she was seeing a psychiatrist about it. Half the outfits she owned didn't even look that good on her and the trick department store mirrors that make you look thinner were an added hindrance to this problem. After ransacking her closet she did eventually find something that didn't look that hideous on her and more importantly than that she had only worn it once so there was a good chance that no one had seen her in it, especially when you consider the fact that she knew none of the guests but she didn't let that interfere with her victory.

Tina searched and searched far and wide for a pair of shoes to go with her outfit but it wasn't quite working out, her dog pretty much chewed up all of them anyway. In the past she had tried to reprimand the dog but it doesn't do any good, they don't understand anything you try to tell them. People always use a common expression about what separates us from the animals but the obvious answer would have to be the power of speech and comprehension skills. Tina wasn't quite sure whether to go out and buy the shoes or change her whole outfit. She realized that something that actually looked good on her was hard to come by so she knew she had to be strong and go out and buy the shoes that matched her near perfect outfit. She called her psychiatrist to lay the proposition on him.

"Hello, may I please speak to Dr Fleming?", Tina asked the secretary who answered the phone.

"I'm sorry but he is with a patient right now, may I give him a message?".

Tina didn't know what to say, she knew that she needed to give this woman a good reason to speak to the doctor and a trivial shopping dilemma just wasn't going to cut it.

"May I please talk to him, I'm on the roof of my building and I swear I'm going to jump unless I get to talk to the doctor", and as she began to say this she opened the window of her apartment in order to hopefully achieve the right sound effects.

"Hold on, I will get him for you", the secretary said in a panicky voice.

"Hello, Dr Fleming here, Tina are you okay? Don't do anything foolish".

As soon as the doctor got on the phone she ditched her phony excuse and started right in with her real concern.

"Well doctor I'm going to a dinner party and it's real important. For various reasons I only have one outfit I can wear but I hardly have any shoes at all, never mind a pair that will go with what I'd be wearing so I think I might have to go shopping for some, what do you think?". There was a short pause as the doctor either considered her plight or thought about hanging up on her after her rather shallow attempt at getting his attention. Even though doctors, especially psychiatrists, were supposed to support their patients and guide them out of temptation in tough times like these, what Tina didn't realize was that her doctor was in actual fact, unbeknownst to her, a closet transvestite (an oxymoron in every sense of the word) so naturally he wanted to help her but he couldn't argue the seriousness of a possible fashion faux-pas.

The next day Tina was out there fighting the madding crowds in the mall in a vain attempt to buy the perfect pair of shoes, weaving in and out of all the stores she set her beady little eyes on, whether they sold shoes or not ceased to be an issue anymore. In her heart of hearts she knew that it was too soon to be shopping again, she started getting short of breath and she could feel her lungs trying to fight off the already stale mall air. The walls of the mall were closing in fast, or so it seemed; she feared that they would swallow her whole if a pair of shoes weren't found quickly. Just as things looked hopeless (which is the perfect place for a positive turn) she ran into a new store called "Elegant Shoes"; it was all right there in the name, no more had to be said, it was a shopping addict's dream come true. She walked into the store and immediately she began looking for that perfect shoe that provided both form and function or was that too much to ask for? She hoped it wasn't but just in case it was she had better get two pairs,

she thought to herself; obviously starting to crack by rationalizing her addiction to shopping. She had almost browsed through the entire store three times over and was getting frustrated with the selection when she came upon her dream shoes and suddenly life seemed good but at the same time bad because after all she was excited about shoes for god's sake which is kind of pathetic but what are you going to do. She took the shoes and a few others she kind of liked and went to sit down in a chair to try them on feeling they would be a perfect fit and she could get out of this mall and the claustrophobic feeling it gave her. No matter how hard she jammed her foot in that shoe it just wasn't going to go and after seriously cramping her foot a couple times she decided to seek the assistance of an employee for a larger size. Getting the attention of someone proved to be quite a feat even though the staff weren't particularly busy so perhaps they could sense she would be trouble. She was finally able to get the attention of a tall, balding man named Sam who seemed to be a manager type, in basic terms, a guy who looked like he had sold a few shoes in his day.

"Do you have this in a size nine?", Tina held up the shoe in nervous anticipation.

"No, I'm really sorry we are totally sold out of that size in that style but we will be getting more in at the end of the week".

Tina thought about it for a minute and then realized that the party was tonight and she wouldn't get the shoes in time and this thought made her angry. The walls were starting to close in on her again, she was getting faint and before she knew it she threw her arm back like she was getting ready to throw a base-ball and beat Sam upside his head with the heel of the shoe. Everyone stood in complete awe at what they had just witnessed. It had almost seemed like a cartoon in the way it happened except that Sam wasn't moving that much, well... in actual fact not at all really. All of this would be fine and dandy if it weren't for the overwhelming fact that Tina still didn't have a pair of shoes.

Car Trouble

Car Trouble

As Allen sat parked on the shoulder of the road he thought about how handy it would have been to have taken some kind of car repair class because now he was stuck and he knew absolutely nothing. Just moments before he was driving quite happily, minding his own business when everything seemed to just stop working at once; needless to say it was very strange. He had only quite recently purchased the car from a friend of his so although it was not new, it was of course, new to him and that is all that mattered at the time because he had only just got his drivers license and was a bit anxious to get on the road. He always kept the thought in the back of his head that he knew nothing about cars and that one day when he owned a car this very thing would happen. His first clue was when he drove his mother's car once and it began to overheat a bit, so he wanted to add some anti-freeze because that's the one thing he did know but he didn't have any and was somewhere where he didn't have access to any but he thought he saw his dad use water once in an emergency. This practice was observed correctly by Allen, but where observation is sharp common sense takes a backseat, because unfortunately when his dad did it, it was really hot but during that particular period they were going through a cold snap (colder than usual) and it all froze solid and he had to get it towed to a garage which felt a bit embarrassing just because there was nothing really wrong with it at all it just needed to be parked inside so it could thaw out. Allen's mother still to this day won't let him drive her car even though her mechanical knowledge is just as lacking (if not more so). Therefore the rule seems to be that you are entitled to screw up your own property as much as you wish which is exactly why Allen's mother isn't expected to show much interest now. Well she might show a little interest just for the simple fact that it would be sweet revenge and better still she didn't have to lift a finger to cause it, so when people try to say that the best revenge is living well they aren't really taking into account that a good physical or emotional crippling can feel pretty darn good too.

A tow truck finally came to pick up Allen's car and as the tow truck driver hooked up his car to the truck a déjà vu feeling began to engulf Allen's thoughts and he felt so stupid because this was the second time this had happened and considering that he had been driving for a very limited time so far it had been a very expensive and un-fun experience. At the garage Allen tried to quickly invent somewhat believable car knowledge so he wouldn't appear stupid when it came to cars in order to give the mechanic the impression that Allen was a shrewd customer and didn't intend on getting ripped off. As it turned out, shrewd or not, the car had many problems and the mechanic told Allen that it would be faster to tell Allen all the things that weren't wrong with the car. Allen was naturally disappointed with the news but chuckled over it a little because this was the way his luck always went, a sign that maybe he was starting to get a bit delirious over how bad his luck really was. Although Allen didn't pay much for the car he realized then that the old adage was true about getting what you pay for but he decided to get the car fixed rather than getting a new one because he did like it a lot. He just made a mental note to kill his friend the next time he saw him, of course he had to hand it to him, he knew when to sell. The problems seemed to grow the more the mechanics rooted around, the exhaust system, the carburetor, the only thing the car seemed to have going for it was that the wheels weren't flat yet but as far as Allen was concerned they might as well be that would be the icing on the cake.

The biggest annoyance from this whole experience was that Allen was going to have to take the bus or a taxi for a while which was no big deal I guess but when he thought about it he couldn't believe how easily you start to rely on your car and it becomes hard to visualize yourself without it and how you got along without it so well in the first place. Dave, the mechanic told Allen that his car would be ready in a few weeks, what with all the things it needed done to it and the lineup of cars that Dave pointed to that seemed to be ahead of his, it was a wonder that it would be ready that soon.

For the next few weeks Allen bided his time by working overtime a couple of nights at the warehouse he worked at in order to pay for the repair work and the rest of the time was filled by attempting to come to grips with the fact that his fiancé of seven months had run away to Las Vegas to marry his brother, it once again put in perspective how important his car was to him. Dave called Allen a few times during the weeks to let Allen know what was going on, how much every procedure would cost and to tell Allen whether he could still drive the car if any particular procedure wasn't done because he knew Allen would be

wanting to save money wherever possible. Dave was a rare find, a sensitive and caring mechanic in tune with Allen's needs.

Dave called Allen when the car was close to being done and told him that it was basically done and to come on in and pick it up. They were just giving it a final once over so that Allen would be completely satisfied. At the garage Dave had Allen's car up on a hoist and Dave was just working on Allen's brakes, he assured Allen that they were fine he was just making sure because Dave believed that you should be proud of what you do and if that meant going that extra mile for a customer so be it. As Allen stood and watched Dave put the final touches on the brakes (putting the wheels back in place and such), Allen quite innocently leaned against the wall where upon he flicked the switch that lowered the hoist and instantly sent the car down on Dave. Another mechanic came running over and quickly pulled Dave out from under the car where he began to apply mouth to mouth resuscitation on the near lifeless looking body. Allen was glad someone was there who knew what to do; as for Allen, he just stood there like a deer trapped in the headlights (something like when his car first broke down). The other people in the garage just looked at Allen in utter disbelief and this made him wonder if this would affect the return of his car.

One Hundred Percent

One Hundred Percent

Steve and his e-bay, it was his life. It was his hobby, and it was his main source of income. He prided himself on what a good e-bayer he was, his attention to detail, his pride in providing such excellent customer service. He had been an e-bay seller since 2001, with an unblemished score of 20,000 soon staring him in the face. And now he was on a plane to confront the person who was responsible for giving him his first dose of negative feedback. As he sat on the plane he thought of all the things he was going to say when he got there. Maybe he was on his way to explain his side of it, maybe he was even making a mistake. All he knew thus far is that when he got his first, as he felt, unfair negative/ "didn't get my stuff", feedback alert, whatever you may call it, he just point blank freaked out. And now, address in hand, found himself on a plane to argue with a complete stranger.

As he explained, quite plainly, in his listings for the last month, he was going to be out of town and would not have access to a computer for awhile and that he hoped everyone understood, and he would mail things out just as soon as he got home. It even went on to mention that "IF YOU DO NOT AGREE WITH THESE TERMS, DO NOT BID." And further went on to mention his 100% standing and the premiere business member he was. But this guy Steve was going to see, this guy was not cool, very uncool indeed. And this guy did eventually get his stuff, but once you have a strike against you it can't be taken back, so Steve didn't know if he wanted an apology?... vengeance?... what? Whatever he wanted, this guy he was going to see lived in Iowa, and Steve lived in Washington State...lots of time for pent up anger to subside. So, whatever he was feeling when he first stepped on that plane, he hoped he could maintain. It would be awful to go all that way and lose sight.

Steve ate and he drank...and he stared at a piece of paper: *Scott Arnold, 1054 Spencer Street Iowa City*. Yup, this was it. It won't be long now, he thought to himself. To maintain Steve's disposition he just kept thinking about that 99%, that would be 100% if it weren't for this e-bay clown. As he drank (as the drinking helped with this) he thought about how he was going to take a taxi right from the airport to the perpetrator's house and simply burn it down, or just throttle him right then and there, and thusly, be home in time for dinner.

When Steve's plane touched down, he was raring to go. What he was going to do was still up in the air, but he hailed a taxi, and off he went. The taxi driver and Steve were both half asleep, but Steve felt uncomfortable just sitting there, so he started up a conversation. It was the usual kind of, "Lovely city you have here", "Where are you from?", "How long have you been driving a taxi?" type of thing. Inevitably, the taxi driver got around to what brought Steve to Iowa City. Steve saw nothing wrong in what he was doing, so he was honest in the reason for his trip. This made the taxi driver perk up a bit, and it did cross his mind to question this, but a fare is a fare so why get involved. Steve had come all this way, and it's not like a taxi driver somewhere was going to say, "but...", and Steve was going to suddenly say, "I see what your saying", and forego his plans just like that.

Upon first approach of the house, Steve was cautious. He got down on his hands and knees, crawled over to the window, raised is head slowly, and peered in. What he saw was a totally nude guy dancing in front of his stereo. Steve lowered his head, turned around, and crawled away. He thought for a few minutes about the best way to proceed; he came a long way, so make no mistake, he was going to proceed. He decided to wait a few minutes, collect himself, and just walk right up to the door, and be as straight forward and direct as he could. Steve was not confrontational by nature, but nevertheless, he let a few minutes pass by, took a few deep breaths, walked up to the door and knocked. A few minutes later a guy with greasy, slicked back hair, a shirt on, and wrapped in a large red towel came to the door, and opened with, "Yeah... What do you want?" Steve scoped the living room (which the front door opened onto), and before he could even respond, he eyeballed a long box in the corner he immediately recognized as something he had packaged; It was a keyboard that was hard to miss due to its length. This stirred something deep within Steve, he wasn't sure what it was exactly, but before he knew it he was barging past the man in the towel to get a better look at the package he recognized.

"Um...CAN I HELP YOU?" the man shouted.

Steve turned to him, "When did you get this package?"

"What is this?", said the man, "a few days ago, not that it is any of your concern". "Oh, but it is", Steve disagreed, " I sent you this package about a week ago, I know because you gave me negative feedback, and claimed you never got it, when, if you had just waited awhile, here it is".

And so the argument started, and went on for sometime. It was very therapeutic for Steve; he wasn't getting anywhere, and it was not going to change anything, and he knew it, but he was, in a weird way, having a blast. Steve picked up the keyboard to check the posting date, the man in the toweled yelled, "Put that down!", and he reached over Steve to try and grab it away. During the turmoil, Steve spun around to face the man with the towel, still clutching on to the long box, and in the process hitting the guy in the back of the head, and knocking him out cold. This panicked Steve so much, that without thinking he hit him in the face again when the guy fell backwards from the first blow. When the guy, now towel-less, fell to the floor, he appeared to be on the dead side. Steve didn't know how to check really, and started to freak out. Steve sat on the couch for awhile wondering what to do. So, he did the only reasonable thing that there was to do in this situation. He grabbed a piece of toilet paper to pick up the receiver on the telephone in the kitchen, phoned a taxi, and got the hell out of there.

Pizza:
Food of the Undesirables

My name is Richard Nyland and I am thirty-one years of age and I deliver pizza for a living. This is not a moonlighting job because my other job pays me too little nor am I doing this in a desperate attempt to work my way through law school - this is what I really do for a living. I am not a stupid man (although people who best know me may hold a different opinion). I am quite sure I could have made something big out of myself and who's to say that I still won't but the fact is that I like delivering pizza. It's true that there is not any real glamour or benefits in the pizza delivery game but sometimes, believe it or not, something will happen that will make me think: Boy, I am sure glad I am delivering pizza tonight. First, I am saving money right off the bat because quite often there is free pizza up for grabs; in part from the boss as a way of, I guess, thanking me for doing such a damn fine job delivering those pizzas and second, pizzas that I get to eat that were the result of "crank calls". If you wished to start delivering pizza yourself but didn't like to eat it (and who in their right mind wouldn't) it is my opinion that you won't enjoy working around pizza as much as me, or at least someone who finds it mildly acceptable. I'm not saying you have to live on it (although I sure could) but it would help things considerably. And here's another little fact that I read about pizza somewhere (I am aware that just because I read it somewhere doesn't make it a fact): it increases your I.Q. In pizza delivery circles this can really come in handy, whether it's making quick change at someone's front door or the rapid hand/eye movement that needs to be used when finding addresses you have never heard of while you drive. Truth be known I did read this pizza making you smarter thing in an gossip news website but it is my belief that it is true because the way I see it is that they only sensationalize the stories about people and things that their readers find interesting, especially if it's juicy gossip, whereas not too many people care either way if pizza makes you smarter or not so there is no need to lie about it, is there? And that is why I think it is the truth. And that's all I have to say about that.

Another advantage to delivering pizza is that all those tips you make are entirely yours. As far as I or any other pizza boy is concerned those are tax-free dollars so when you are delivering that pizza lay it on thick and don't be afraid to kiss some ass. Speaking of kissing ass; sex is not that uncommon a thing to have come up when delivering a pizza. It's still a long way off from being common place of course but it does happen. And if this should occur and you are wondering what to do; you can stop that wondering right now...you have the sex and then it's business as usual. If you think that you are ever being disloyal to your boss for a second you can get that thought out of your head right now because as far as I am concerned (which I know doesn't really amount to anything) you are going above and beyond the call of duty to ensure that the customer is a satisfied customer so Godspeed to you. As far as people who morally oppose this type of business relation I honestly don't know what to tell you, I guess you can feel pretty good about the fact that you didn't allow yourself to be compromised but I can almost guarantee that you don't feel half as good as I do knowing what I did. Aside from that the only "real " problem before you is if the person you delivered to is married and is their better half going to be coming through the door any minute; in which case it becomes just like any bad seventies teenage movie that you've ever seen.

There have been a few times where women that I have delivered pizza to were single mothers with their children in the same room with us and that's where it tends to get a little tacky for even me so now I always have to carry around some sort of toy or stuffed animal in my car to keep them occupied. And chances are if you delivered pizza you wouldn't be married because if you are anything like me you are in your thirties and you are a pizza boy and from the research I've done I can tell you that, in general, women don't find this all that intriguing. Maybe you are some sort of aspiring artist who is just doing this until your "big break" comes or maybe you are already big but you are artistically blocked right now and need to take a step back and reflect and find some sort of inspiration. Well if that doesn't describe delivering pizza I don't know what does. If you do ever wish to break into the pizza delivery biz I can say in all honesty that you will meet some great people and get some great stories out of it that will bring you out of your creative slump in no time if you are indeed in one, if not it will take a little longer.

Just to give you an idea of what I mean I once delivered pizza to a guy who answered the door completely naked. I know this sounds like a common story and could be considered an urban legend but the weird part of the story was that he wanted me to come into his house and feed it to him while he sat in this adult high chair sort of thing, it was swimming in weirdness. I would have obliged but lots of pizzas were being ordered that night so it was real busy, besides, for that I was going to have to charge him extra and I have no idea how much a gigolo makes these days but I wasn't quite ready to break into that business just yet. Although, I'm sure that is something that pizza companies could look into. I am sure there is no legal way of doing it but if they could I bet the pizza companies would make a killing and it would give a whole new meaning to customer service.

Something that I have learned through the years though is that customers can be very deceitful in that ordering pizza is just a cover up for something more sinister. Yes it's true; major (or minor) religious groups are now phoning in pizza orders just so they can preach the gospel to unsuspecting pizza boys. I think the practice is pretty underhanded but I can respect it because just like a business they can see that their numbers are down and they need to try anything they can to entice more customers, or in their case followers. If you do fall into their trap I can only urge you to stay and listen to their spiel (whether you agree with it or not) because you will most likely receive a big fat tip. But in the likely event you don't receive one don't hurt them because it was probably your fault for sounding too interested thus they probably thought that them saving a lonely pizza boy from the bowels of hell was thanks enough . I don't want to give you the wrong idea though; if you are interested in what they have to say by all means give them a contribution and take the reading material that they offer but for God's sake with all that God talk going on don't let them disrespect the pizza. Maybe bring it up in the conversation somewhere like: "you know I think Jesus ate pizza." Which I think is a nice thought but that's just because I like it so much that it seems right somehow. Besides there is nothing that really disproves that he didn't eat it, I mean most of the bible is based on hearsay anyway so there you go.

I can remember the time when I delivered a pizza to someone and it was the wrong kind and he pulled a gun on me. Delivering pizza isn't really considered a dangerous occupation but just to be safe always check to ensure that it's the right kind before you leave. If it does turn out to be the wrong kind turn to the person who made it and say something like "hey, you made the wrong kind" and if they give you any friction over it you would do good to mention that your good friend Richard was almost shot over something like this.

So back to this gun situation: it was the wrong kind of pizza and he flipped out which was really scary but I got out of it by employing the time honored tradition of pleading and begging which surprisingly enough worked. When he let me go I was so happy to get out of there that I wasn't going to think anymore about it but then he didn't pay me for the pizza (wrong or not) so I had to turn him in. I found out later that the reason why he did it was that he had just lost his job as a florist that day and I guess that this wrong pizza thing was the last straw, actually the very last straw was probably me laughing at the fact that he had been a florist (he was a big, rough looking guy you see). But as he explained to me while he had a gun to my head there was once a time when he was secure enough in his masculinity to follow his dream of becoming a florist no matter what his friends with their macho insecurities might say.

Something else I should say before I forget is before you present the pizza to the customer you shouldn't sneeze or cough on the pizza unless you know who you are delivering it to and you dislike them. Note: know your enemies and be sure that you are going to their address before you do something you will regret later.

Something that I have not explained yet is that up to now I have only referred to the pizza delivery guys and not the girls (in fact I'm sure that if you had been reading this in front of me you would have asked me about that) and this is because I have never seen or heard of one. I'm certainly not saying that they don't exist, they probably do, somewhere. All I am saying is that I don't know of any pizza delivery women and none of them work where I work. In fact it's really weird when you think about it because you would think that women need to earn money somehow (they're like men that way) and delivering pizza is a pretty decent ways of doing so; at least in my opinion it is. It's possible that my job is a terrible one and I just don't know it yet in which case it's a good thing that there are people like me around to do the crappy jobs that no one else wants to do. I have given this some thought (because I had nothing better to do) and could only come to the conclusion that since women mature faster than men and on average seem more sensible (the second part of that thought is solely my opinion) maybe they feel that delivering pizza is demeaning and not worth their female capabilities. Although if that were really the case what does that say about men?

I did at one time have an opportunity to deliver five pizzas to a party that consisted of the host and lots of life size cardboard cut-outs of guests, it was really sad. He invited me to stay for awhile, which I did because he was my last delivery of the night and I didn't want to be rude although I must say I was extremely tired so I wasn't going to be much company but when I took a look around and saw what I had to compete with I figured that even if I fell asleep I would be shades above everyone else. When my host saw that I appeared to be a little stand-offish at the sight of this large group of figures he came over to me and goaded me into mingling with them. I tried the best I could but I felt like an idiot and there is only so much you can say. All and all they were boring and too one-dimensional; I even fancied someone and tried to pick her up but she just ignored me.

Earlier this evening my brother Peter called me up at work and invited me to a Thanksgiving party at his house which I accepted because it just so happened I wasn't doing anything special but I told him that just for the record I could have been doing something. That's when I could have sworn I heard a big snorty laugh come over the receiver of the phone; he denies it but I heard something. During our phone conversation he tells me to bring enough pizza for about twelve guests which I will gladly do except we spend the next twenty minutes arguing about whether twelve pizzas is too many or too few, which means we have to count off each guest and try to examine their girth and how it relates to pizza. When I enquire as to why his wife Lorie isn't making turkey this year like every other year he tells me that she is away visiting relatives and he can't cook a turkey which isn't surprising because he's an idiot who doesn't even know enough to ask for help. He later tells me that he knew that pizza was a terrible idea on Thanksgiving but he left the food planning to the very last minute, the last minute being right now, and it was too late to cancel the party. Peter told me that the party was at eight so I told him that I would go there at around nine as I just had to deliver this one pizza and then I would be ready to go. After I hung up the phone I wondered why it always seemed as though people were only nice to me and invited me to parties when they wanted something from me and still I did it, gee I'm a nice guy.

Before I went to Peter's that night I did go and make that last delivery I had to make but it took a bit more time than I had anticipated. When I got to the house I was delivering to I could hear what sounded like fighting coming from inside but couldn't really pick up what was going on and I was going to wait patiently until it stopped but it never did so I rang the doorbell. When the door bell sounded the yelling stopped and I heard someone yell "pizzas here!" and with that the door slowly opened. I was greeted by two gentlemen with hoods over their heads with two eye holes cut out of them so that they could see me and because pizza boys are good deducers of the obvious, I figure that they are the tenants of the house trying to have a laugh at the expense of the delivery guy. But I soon find out they are burglars, and I had just interrupted them while they were applying their trade, which from the looks of it they were doing quite well, in my opinion. I took one look at the guns that were swaying in the breeze at their sides and I did the next logical thing I could think of: I immediately tell them that I was sorry for the mix up but that I think I delivered this pizza to the wrong address. They assure me that I didn't but as I continue to look at the guns they are toting I try to re-assure them that I did. We go on at some length about this until they point their guns in the direction of my face, and that is when I come around to their way of thinking.

They tell me to slowly put the pizza on the table and step away. One of the gun men remains holding a gun to my head while the other one checks the box to see if I did in fact bring the right pizza. They inform me that I did good but accuse me of trying to knowingly take back the pizza when I knew it was the right one all along, and they launch into some story about how robbing people can really build up an appetite. I swear to them that I thought it was the wrong one and, quite convincingly I think, try to testify as to the magnitude of my own stupidity, hoping that they show mercy towards an aging pizza delivery boy. They both agree that there is not much that is sadder than that and they inquire as to how someone like myself has the self respect to do this at my age. I tell them that that is a sore point with me and that I don't really wish to discuss it. They tell me that they understand and drop that entire line of questioning.

The woman who owns the house (or maybe she rents, I guess it's not really important) is tied up in the corner and she struggles to wave at me. I don't know her but I think that it is a pleasant enough gesture to wave at a stranger, especially in her position, so I wave back. I asked the armed men if they knew it was Thanksgiving because it wasn't exactly a big night for ordering pizza. They told me that that was the best night to rob people as usually they are out eating turkey somewhere, and that it was a big shock when they found that the owner (or renter) of this house was home, and then they told me to shut up. I tell them that this was my last delivery of the night and that now I am going to my brothers for Thanksgiving dinner and that now I am running a little late and that I really had to go. The burglars didn't see it my way though and proceeded to discuss the possibilities of tying me up as well. They agreed that they would and I thought that they shouldn't but as it turned out I didn't get a vote, and when they asked me if I would rather be tied up or shot it made me feel all that much better about their decision. In a last ditch effort to try to escape I offered them more pizza I had in the car that I was actually taking to the Thanksgiving party and to further entice them I told them that it was cooked in the form of a turkey, which it was. They declined the offer but could have sworn that I just questioned people having pizza on Thanksgiving when I was about to do the same thing. I told them that we were going to have turkey but for whatever reason my brother phoned me at the last minute and told me to bring pizza and I also reminded them that it was in the form of a turkey. They told me that it didn't matter what it looked like, that pizza

is pizza and they explained that now that they had caught me being hypocritical that there was no question that they were going to have to tie me up.

As they move in on me I spring into my fighting stance, I grab both of them and fling them around the room a couple times and then bash their heads against the wall repeatedly. And then with what I picked up at delivery boy defense class I inflict a series of devastating manoeuvres (which I can't divulge to the reader as I am sworn to secrecy) that render them helpless. After which I proceed to untie the girl; she thinks I am the greatest thing since sliced bread and I tell her to tell me something I don't know. I start to tie the robbers up and wait for the police to get there; I keep the masks on the robbers' heads so the police can tell who is who. As we wait for the police to get there I tell the men tied up on the floor that they owe me $17.50 and they assure me they are good for it but it doesn't look promising.